*What's remarkable is the degree to which
Americans have distrusted silence and its parent
condition, stillness [...]. The daydreaming child, or
daydreaming adult, is usually an object of contempt
or therapy.*
          —Charles Baxter, "Stillness"

I fell in love with people sleeping.
          —Daniel Johns, "Across the Night"

Arguments for
Stillness

poems by

ERIK CAMPBELL

A Curbstone/Rattle Edition
Curbstone Press

A CURBSTONE / RATTLE EDITION
funded by the Frieda C. Fox Foundation

Printed in the U.S. by BookMobile
Cover design: Stone Graphics
Cover image: "La condition humaine" by René Magritte; Gift of
Collectors Committee, National Gallery of Art, Washington DC, 1933;
oil on canvas.

This book was published with the support of the
Frieda C. Fox Foundation in collaboration with
Rattle magazine, with supplemental support
provided by the Connecticut Commission on
Culture and Tourism.

Library of Congress Cataloging-in-Publication Data

Campbell, Erik, 1972-
  Arguments for stillness / by Erik Campbell.— 1st ed.
    p. cm.
  ISBN-10: 1-931896-26-7 (pbk. : alk. paper)
  ISBN-13: 9781931896269
  I. Title.

  PR9500.9.C36A89 2006
  821'.92—dc22

                                        2005032719

published by
CURBSTONE PRESS   321 Jackson St.   Willimantic, CT 06226
     phone: 860-423-5110   e-mail: info@curbstone.org
                   www.curbstone.org

ACKNOWLEDGMENTS

The author wishes to thank the magazines where some of these poems were first published:
"Consider What Passes for Kindness These Days" and "The Subtle Again" were published in *The Iowa Review*;
"Poem for Neil Postman," "Considering Metal Man (as a Template for World Peace)," "Poet and Audience," "The Man Kissed the Letter," "Hamlet: The Action Figure Series," and "Mysterious Farang" were published in *Rattle*;
"The Fortunate Man," "Nietzsche Dancing," and "The Magic Mountain" were published in *Nimrod International Journal*;
"The Revolt" was published in *Confrontation*;
"How to Appreciate Art" was published in *Bogg*;
"Smoking Is Not an Activity" and "Lesson" were published in *The Oklahoma Review*;
"Familiarity," "Herr Samsa, before Gregor's Death," and "About the Type" were published in *New Delta Review*;
"Strongbox" was published in *Poetry Motel*;
"Dead Man's Wallet" was published in *Tin House*;
"I Watched *Frankenstein*" was published in *Cranky*;
and "The Redemption of Tantalus" was published in *The Virginia Quarterly Review*.

With deep appreciation and gratitude to my careful, helpful readers and editors: Dr. A.G. Hartman, Tim Green, Alan Fox, Stellasue Lee, Sandy Taylor, Judith Doyle, William Kloefkorn, Ted Genoways, and P. Scott Stanfield.

For Shari

CONTENTS

III Still Lives

IV East

Foreword

My advice: Don't enter these poems if you want to exit unchanged. Consider, for example, what Gregor's father says in "Herr Samsa, before Gregor's Death": "Thank your goddamn maker that you / Never sired a metaphor. Be happy / You're not surrounded by connotations. // As if the literal world ain't tough / Enough as it is. Or it isn't."

Erik Campbell confronts the literal world from angles both fresh and expansive. A young man who spent his formative years in Nebraska, USA, he wrote these poems while experiencing a self-imposed exile in the jungles and mountains of Papua, Indonesia, a place that, according to my atlas, is more than a stone's throw away from Omaha or Lincoln or the Sandhills. He worked and read and wrote, contemplated and sketched and taught for several years until *Arguments for Stillness* at last evolved. Thus the "arguments" have been carefully thought through and crafted; they reflect a sensibility that manages to find stillness in a world that often makes little distinction between melody and cacophony. I especially appreciate his use of "arguments" in the title; it suggests that stillness does indeed need a defender—which probably in fact it does, though in theory most of us would no doubt agree that occasional stillness is at least desirable and at most absolutely necessary. That is, when we take time to consider such things, amidst the din of our daily, digitized lives.

Campbell was a student of mine several years ago at Nebraska Wesleyan University. Even then his writing had a freshness that compelled and challenged and delighted his peers—as well as his slack-jawed professor; it was, and is, a brightness derived from a voice both incisive and pragmatic. Consider, for example, these lines from "Lesson": "...true sadness / Consists of those things you will never have / A chance to miss. Your life, he insists, will end / Up on your quiz; your life *is* the quiz. Please // Don't fuck this one up."

If this collection is the blockbuster I believe it to be, Erik Campbell is far from screwing this one up. He offers the reader many arguments for stillness, each an investigation to mediate, each an inducement to consider more than one side of any proposition. His subjects and settings range from what passes for kindness in Waterloo, Nebraska, to what might be viewed as monstrous in Chiang Mai, Thailand. Time and again he hits the nail squarely on its vulnerable head: "And I felt suddenly as shameless / As a man in a bar teaching / A pretty woman to shoot pool." Yes, indeed. And anyone who doesn't understand or feel the depth of such shamelessness has spent far too much time in Sunday school.

Campbell has said that he wrote many of the first drafts of these poems while living at a mine site "on some days working at 10,000 feet, wearing a hard hat and safety boots, between one of the last equatorial glaciers in the world and an enormous open pit mine that's almost two kilometers wide." In such a context the poet must surely have come to appreciate the importance of remoteness and contemplation. It isn't surprising, then, that his arguments ring true. In the face of "the whole exploding world" the poet finds a measure of solace in peace and stillness.

No doubt these distinctive poems were influenced significantly by the work he does for a large mining company, from his living several years cloistered in a jungle, and by other places and events: the Bali and Jakarta bombings, living in Thailand for a spell, living in Indonesia for a longer spell, wandering wide-eyed around Egypt and Cambodia, considering American life and culture from without—all helped to inscribe and transform Campbell's felt experience and made their way explicitly and implicitly into the poems. To read the poems is to become aware of the depth of the poet's own awareness of happenings both near and remote.

Pay close attention to the poems, then, and you will be rewarded; they will tease and startle you into doing some serious thinking, but they also will delight you with their wryness, their compelling connections, and their occasional audacity, a boldness that strikes me as being a perfectly human extravagance, one that the reader would be wise to enjoy no less than abide. And the Pharaoh in "The Pharaoh Speaks" does not disagree, saying that "History's finishing jest // Is this: She always forgives / Man's extravagances; she celebrates / The shameless in song. Time // Is long. Your smooth economies / Will go unnoticed. In time / Everything still standing is forgiven."

These songs, and the voice that delivers them, are too resonate to be ignored. I look forward to hearing them again—then again and again.

William Kloefkorn
Nebraska State Poet

September, 2005

Prologue:

Considering Metal Man
(as a Template for World Peace)

"The sum of evil would be greatly diminished if men
could only learn to sit quietly in their rooms."
                                        —Blaise Pascal

He sits in Union Square so that you don't have to,
Covered in metallic paint, not moving, like applied

Pascal taken one step publicly further. The tourists
Patronize him, put money in his gold painted fedora,

And encourage him not to explain. The homeless wish
They had his strangeness, his calculation, his economy

Of gesture. The writers know he is a fleshed out character
Worthy of 200 pages or more, a catatonic knight-

Errant appearing everywhere in full armor.
The philosophers see him as a meta-symbol,

A shimmering sage who sits better than the Buddha.
Look how he sits and stares, they say. Observe how

Nobody dies because of this.

I

Potential Energies

Hamlet: The Action Figure Series

"Our wills and fates do so contrary run
That our devices still are overthrown:
Our thoughts are ours, their ends none of our own."
III.ii.206-208

I
HAMLET AND OPHELIA

Jason is upset, downright melancholic,
That Amy won't let Ophelia die.
It isn't a matter of misreading the text,
She says, but of transcending it with love:
Of justice being served. In short, Ophelia
Didn't get what she deserved.

She tells Jason that he can quote
Coleridge all he wants. *This* Ophelia
Is getting married in a proper church
Wedding to a man who occasionally
Wears pastels, speaks to her
Directly in lieu of soliloquizing,
Unpacks his heart without metaphor,
And never mentions her nonexistent lisp.

(Jason later appealed these libelous
Liberties to his parents while they
Were watching *American Idol.* "Play
Nice," they said, without irony.)

And with no bare bodkin in sight
Jason locked himself in his room,
Made an artificial night.

"He's become a real piece of work,"
Jason's parents told their shrink.
"We think he thinks too deeply.

Or maybe drugs."

II

ROSENCRANTZ AND GUILDENSTERN
   (*Figures Come With Detachable,
   Interchangeable Heads*)

It wasn't, as one might have expected,
The doltish or indifferent children
Who understood them,

But the Existentialists in the rough
Who didn't yet have words
To articulate their ennui; those kids

Who'd sampled Stoppard, owned
Every *They Might Be Giants* CD,
And wore T-shirts that read:
"Years of therapy have taught me
That nothing is my fault."

No one knows how they play
With their figures, much less if
They play nice. It's rumored

That they don't play with them at all.
Only stare at them, at their plastic heads

Resting at their molded feet,
Waiting for Act V to arrive.

III
THE GRAVE-DIGGER

With seven proofs of purchase
You could send away
For a limited edition Grave-

Digger, yet the company
Only produced six different figures
(Rosencrantz and Guildenstern
Came typically together). The clever

Kids got the joke straight away
And punned those kids who
Purchased two Poloniuses
(And later received a box
Of air in the mail)
To death.

IV
HORATIO

Because he wasn't passion's slave
Few kids knew what to do with him
(And so Horatio was dangerous to own).

He appealed to the noncommittal
Because he scarcely did anything
But stand there, barely breathing,
Always listening, never passing
Judgments that weren't
First whispered in Hamlet's ear.

Marcos bought his Horatio
When he and Jason were still
Best friends. Since Jason's been

Locked away, tinkering with his
Epitaph, both Marcos and Horatio
Have had trouble existing.

V

POLONIUS (*Unbound*)

It wasn't at all strange that the Polonius figure
Was ignored by the children and purchased
By the adults with New Historicist proclivities.

They were tired of seeing him
Lampooned on stage and in film, reduced
By directors so egregiously to
Neither a borrower nor a lender be.

Polonius's fans well knew that he never believed
In *to thine own self be true*, and in lieu of this,

Emphasized the first scene in Act II, where Polonius
Meets with Reynaldo in a locked room and shows
What a shrewd father he is. The cult of Polonius

Wants justice done, akin to what T.S. Eliot did
For John Donne. They demand full restitution;
They insist on secular resurrection.

VI
CLAUDIUS

Those children old enough
To occasion the morning paper
Or glance at CNN of course

Chose Claudius and never rounded out
The action figure series. They couldn't

Find sense in surrounding Claudius
With the non ambitious or, worse yet,
The satiated. In their version of the play

There is no Act V. Claudius is forever
Taking meetings, making mergers.
Gertrude is pushed to the periphery
Of the stage—one highlighted name
In his PDA, among many.

Hamlet's been sent packing, safely
Stowed in military school since Act II.

Claudius owns Denmark, Norway,
And you.

Winchester Mansion

If anyone on the outside asked, they would only smile
And shake their heads, silently affirming that ghosts, like sins,
Are a private business. And if there was no logic in the house,

There was smooth certainty in the wages. "We have years of better
Than even pay," they would say if pressed. "Call it lunatic work
If you please." They had all been privy to Mrs. Winchester's genius,

Those mornings she would appear with plans scribbled on paper
Napkins or the back of dust jackets, last minute revisions
And decisions from a besieged architect's hand. "Can you build

This?" she would ask the foreman, "because it seems impossible
Enough to me." But more than her money they respected her sense
Of dread; the only wealthy woman they'd ever met who thought

Herself capable of death, the sole patron who commissioned sublime
Illusions of functionality and encouraged the carpenters to stop making
Sense. Some days she would lose herself in her house, and it was then

That she was happiest, finding herself suddenly, say, on a spiral
Staircase leading to a ceiling. The carpenters would hear her laughter
At lunchtime (the only time the building stopped) adumbrating up

Blind chimneys and off of trap doors, hinting at certain sundry truths
That they would need to leave their lunches again to find. Perhaps
No end is the end when building a metaphor, or there is no need

For locks when all the doors lead nowhere. The foolish try
To escape their sins; the wise give them rooms of their own.

Consider What Passes for Kindness These Days

The farmers in 1942 Waterloo, Nebraska,
Would meet at the train tracks,
Their hands shoved deep and final
In their overalls fingering lint, always lint.

My father would stand with his father
Whose withered arm hung limp at his side,
His right hand in his pocket like the other
Complete, incomplete men, and wait

With them for the train to slow through town
In a coughing arc where the men were poised,
Their hands exhumed for the gathering
Of coal that the hoboes would throw,

Scooping it out, handfuls of black hail, yawping
With beneficence, pleased with their work.
The farmers would scurry about the tracks still
Ringing from the weight; they understood

Each other's faces, the small acts that were beyond
Shame when one had warmth. My father would
Gather as his father would give a good-armed wave
To the hoboes, shouting above the train whistle.

Call it another day of heat, with coal in pockets,
Everything chalky black. Hands at their sides,
Collars up, not quite slouching the warm walk home.

Headache

He said, "Listen to me. Remember
To do everything tenderly."

"My father had a withered arm,"
He said, "His left, so he had to use
His right for everything,
And when he hit me, he hit me hard
With that arm, so hard I'd have
Headaches for days.
One day your uncle
Al left the cows out
By accident, and since Al
Wasn't around my father hit me
So hard with that arm
That I spun to the ground,
And there was this *sound*
Like something
Breaking, like someone
Somewhere was at the end
Of their rope. Twelve years old
And the next thing I know
He's clutching his head like it
Needed cracking, so I took him
Inside as he pummeled my face,
My arms, screaming, 'My head, my
Head, my fucking head…'

We had to tie him to the bed.

And later the doctor said,
Standing over his body:
'Brain aneurysm. A great deal

Of pain.' I remember how small
He seemed. How quiet and small.

Do you see?" my father said,
"It wasn't his conscience
That killed him."

Nietzsche, Dancing

"Apparently he was given to outbursts
of expressionistic dancing while in the asylum."
—Robert Solomon

It was only later that he tried,
Once he thought all was understood,
After he no longer knew he had buried

Wagner, had all the Gentiles shot. Imagine
The nurses in the asylum late at night,
Surrounding him in his slippers and robe,

Watching him pirouette like a string-less
Marionette. They want him to take his medicine
And *stop it*, but now, sick from words, Nietzsche

Only wants movement. How could they not *see it*,
This final harmlessness? And there is Nietzsche
On stage once again, despite appearances choosing

His steps carefully; if the infinite repetitions
Begin he can keep this up forever. This is a good

Dance, Nietzsche is certain. Look, everyone's
Joining in. Please, come closer, he says.
Dance. It's *only music.*

Herr Samsa, before Gregor's Death

Found himself more and more often
On a certain barstool in Czechoslovakia
Becoming tedious to the regulars who
Drank largely to escape their ironies.

He sat mumbling under his breath
Grunts which, when parsed into words,
Sounded like *thorax* or *pesticide.*
And when he'd finally slap the bar top

And say, "Let me tell you about
My son," the regulars would study
The sweat rings on the bar, or their hands.
"How would you feel if, one day,
You came home and suddenly your son
Was a difficult-to-explain allegory?

What would your neighbors—
Or your *God*—think of that?" This,
Or a derivation thereof, was recently
The question; the answer always
A nodding or shaking of silent heads.

"Be thankful," Gregor's father would say,
Sighing his way toward the door,
"Thank your goddamn maker that you
Never sired a metaphor. Be happy
You're not surrounded by connotations.

As if the literal world ain't tough
Enough as it is. Or it isn't."

Poem for Neil Postman

It's happened Neil,
This poem is proof
You are indeed a prophet.

I saw the verdict
Last night on television.

It was 101 degrees last night
And on channel 26
All the cattle in the world
Were dying,

And suddenly
There was Alex Trebek
On an info-mercial,
Pimp-like and slick,
Trying to sell me
(Can you believe it?)
The Classics.

A different classic
On a different tape, each
Just under 45 minutes.

"If you're like me"
Trebek said,
"You can't seem to find
The time to sit down
And read a classic like
The Iliad,

But with this special offer
You'll be able to sit back

And relax as one of the classics
Is read to you
By such celebrated personalities as:

Paris Hilton (*Hamlet*),
Brad Pitt (*The Idiot*),
Joan Rivers (*Notes from the Underground*),
Elizabeth Taylor (*The Cantos*),
Charlton Heston (*The Antichrist*),
Nicolas Cage (*The Man Without Qualities*),
Just to name a few...

Each classic neatly and coherently
Abridged
So as to run just under an hour.

So
Enrich your life
With a long deserved foundation
In The Classic Literary Tradition

For the low,
Low price of $29.99 a month
For 23 months!"

"Come now," I think I hear
Him say, "you can afford it!

Faust paid less!"

And then Trebek went on
To expound upon the virtues
Of a classical education
And how it makes him
A ready wit
In dinner conversation—

So
I threw the ashtray
Through the television screen
And drafted a formal surrender
To the cosmos
In rhyming blank verse;
Walking to the post office
I thought to myself

It's all this heat
It makes the shit smell worse,

And after I mail this surrender
I think I'll go home and burn
All of my books
So there won't be any evidence,
Any proof when they come for me,

Except for
Of course
This poem

Which I would pay
At least $29.99

To have read to me
Abridged or un
Over and over
By Kato Kaelin

Before seeing how well
The oven fits my head.

Heaven: A Definition

For Neil Postman (1932-2003)

I hope that you will regard Heaven as just another
Bad argument, and carefully avoid Saint Peter

And his crafty, semiotic archangels. Make your way
To the back of Heaven's gates, the servant's entrance

Near the fiery chariot's metaphorical garage. Ask
That disdainful angel smoking a cigarette (the one

That looks like Beckett but isn't) to define Heaven
—no metaphysical diction allowed—and supply

Textual authority. As he ponders, takes a drag,
And scratches his left wing, resist the irony

Of asking after Wittgenstein's health and tell the angel
You would appreciate an audience with Death

Because it's always been your favorite abstraction.
Wait until he is bemused, his brow furrowed

Into cuneiform-like folds of luminous skin, then begin
Your descent. Head straight for NYU and nod livingly

To your secretary. Tell her that classes will resume
Tomorrow and that only the baffled need attend;

Those students who confuse fact with truth can,
Frankly, go to Hell. And for Heaven's sake, don't

Answer the phone or the door. Tell her: "I'll be
In my office, with the door locked, noticing things."

The Revolt

Some of them were caught mid-
Sentence.

They tried to explain their actions,
Their preoccupation with metaphor
(Nothing was ever what it is with them,
Everything chronically like something else),
Their penchant for gazing out of windows,
But Plato would have none of it.

(Some of them were on a walking tour
Of Greece when it happened, and when
They returned and heard no singing
They knew something was out of the air.)

And so the poets were banished, but they
Were together, planning the revolution,
Arguing over its cadence; it took them years
To plot and ponder and memorize their plans,
A few more years to make them rhyme.

And when, in sweetly metered time,
They mobilized their motley forces
And stormed The Republic all chagrin
And allegory, they found Plato writing
A dialogue and felt conflicted,

Wanting to accuse him of mischief or artifice.
But they could only stand there at least
Thrice removed, not feeling
Their victory, scarcely noticing
Their fortunate redundancy.

The Redemption of Tantalus

In lieu of the breakfast I knew he couldn't
Chew, we spent the morning smelling

Brief flowers and giving a try at dangling
Our agonies to passers by.

"I've never *really* minded my situation,"
He clarified for the sake of all exaggerated

Tortures. "It's always been the impossible,
Those Keats-like *almosts* that I find

So sublime. The water still dries at the touch
Of my lips, and yes, the grapes still

Wither on the vine. But my cousin in Crete
Wrote me last week saying I've since become

An adjective *and* a verb. And now, Sisyphus,
Lonely, proper noun that he is, is too jealous

To push—all of Hades is envious. Such stuff
Fills my stomach; such things satisfy my thirst.

Waiting Room

The dentist says it's not your fault, the child's mother said.
You didn't have good water when you were young.

But it should have been like lightning, the child thought,
This too-sudden misery. Or like her little brother, who, still-
Born, never had a name to blame, instead of another

Arcane addition to the long list of reasons for the way
That things are: *bad water* from some bitter, spiteful
Aquifer reserved for the young to drink of.

We watch as her world suddenly becomes a Dystopia,
Like those of the adolescent fiction she pours over;
She, the hesitant heroine, ill-equipped to save the day

Because of a prophecy that presaged bad teeth at nine,
Shameful acne likely from sixteen until her twenties;
The in-between days full of more unfair hours
Than even the strongest, most resilient heroine
Could hope to fill with justice or redemption.

Fuck you, Fluoride, for taking your sweet time.
Fuck everything that takes too long to arrive.

And in her face we're witness to little empires failing
Long before they fall, future loves lacerated
By geography and time, more chances ruined
In the womb. But we don't console.

In time, she's moved from the solipsistic
To the conspicuous, noting that everyone
In the waiting room is watching. She squints

Through the man sitting across from her not reading
His magazine who, she's certain, were he so much younger,

Would never kiss her minefield mouth. This blameless mouth
That only just knew good water; this devastated mouth,
No more to her now than a fraction of a face
Which he would never whisper beautiful.

The Fortunate Man

He knew the state of the miracle
In the mechanical age, and it made him
Sad; too many things lacked meaningful

Shapes, and he suspected that all most people
Really needed were words, portentously timed,
Graciously indefinite. So in an alley in Chinatown,

San Francisco he fills and folds fortune cookies,
Still warm from baking, and where I counted
300 variations on fate, from the innocuous:

"You will be wealthy and wise," to the strange
Specificity of: "You will visit the pyramids
Of Giza." And it was strange for me to see

So many naked pieces of prophecy resting
In barrels, waiting for sweetness and meaning's
Expectant nudge. But the fortune man

Has no trouble with prophecy, he knows
There are 300 ways his future could run;
He's imagined them all already, tweaked

Every platitude for a possible past. His favorite
Fortune reads: "When one lacks a sense of awe
There will be disaster." He finds this notion

Comforting and increases its probability
As he fills and folds because he just can't help
Himself. He keeps this fortune in his wallet

Like a phone number he might someday need,
A photograph of a woman that makes him feel
Beautiful, or a prayer to a multi-purpose saint.

It's because of this he tries to always be amazed.

II

Moments of Stasis

Epistemology

It's like when you listened to The Rolling Stones'
Beggar's Banquet, alone in that hotel hot tub. You
Were newly married, god-like, and drinking champagne

At 10 A.M. with the door open enough to see her sleeping.
You decided then: *We must remember those things*
That make other things be; we must remember how we know.

Like you hoping her dreams were the contented kind,
Accompanied by a soundtrack that sounded
Like a Mick Jagger who loved her, really loved her,

Who married her on a beach in Bali, much like you
Did (only without the beach) short hours before.
That morning, certainly, every moment worth

Keeping benefited from sound (the next morning
You weren't so sure). It's like how the spring of '89
Will always be a certain high school dance, another

Near miss on the list of things you wish you'd chanced,
The very reason lilacs smell like surrender. And tonight
Let's guess that you're angry with her. You don't think

She ever understood her sleeping in that hotel bed,
Or you watching her, toasting her. Were you to bother
With this poem tonight it just wouldn't work right,

Too irresponsibly unbound from your history
Of necessary preludes and contextual requisites;
This poem, or any other, would bore, perhaps

Ruin you. Admit it, while you think it's true,
That most joys, most poems and songs, are projections
Of intention misshapen in translation. Just consider

What might not have happened hadn't your brother
Given you that copy of *The Catcher in the Rye*
Shortly after saying: "I stole this book for you today."

And suppose you're willing to have truck with histories
Other than your own. If so, consider remembering
Certain men in the 17ᵗʰ century, those mendicants,

Monks, and fortunate Faylasufs who died before
The Enlightenment, all of them with a lyrical scientist's
Fervent, inflexible certainty. They had only to look up

At one of seven Heavens to find sense and suggestions
Of order, fixed, inexorable, everywhere applicable,
And die so knowingly before time proved them wrong.

I Watched *Frankenstein*

And later, in perhaps a cliché
Dream, I seem to look right in black
And white. And in this particular

Movie I am neither the wide-eyed
Scientist nor the ineffectual,
Invariably good, and colorless
Leading man. I am the lurching

Beast, bizarrely pausing for flowers,
Wilting them with my fusty breath,
Grunting about this European village
And confusing the villagers' jeers
For cheers, not noticing that everyone
Has a torch save for me. You see,

This monster's foolish enough
To think he's leading a parade.

How to Appreciate Art

Firstly, find the most beautiful
Person in the room, choose
Based on how their face
Translates when they see
A certain painting.

Secondly, follow them
From room to room, mindful
Of what they pause for,
Where they find awe.

Do this enough times
That someone can follow *you*,
Until everyone's a spy
With a sublime agenda

Roving about the gallery.

The Man Kissed the Letter

The man kissed the letter slowly
Before dropping it in the mailbox.

It felt awkward dropping
My gas bill in after this.

Even my packet of poems
Couldn't help, whittled down
To imprecise love letters,
Photocopied for any and all comers.

And I felt suddenly as shameless
As a man in a bar teaching
A pretty woman to shoot pool.

This is nothing new to you.

You've seen the man
Kissing the letter.

Perchance you've been the man
In the bar. As for me,

Anymore I'll take any scrap of shame
That the Greeks left us.

Stopping for Cigarettes

"Sobbing signifies a break-down in communication. [...] Proust
believed his memory retained that which just the same escaped.
Memory completely reveals what presence made off with, though
perhaps only for a time. In a sense it's true to say human sobbing
gives a faint foretaste of eternity."
— Georges Bataille

That I first thought the beautiful, young black woman
Crying into the receiver was keeping the romance
Of the payphone alive probably betrays too much

Of my species of absurdity; the idea that she wanted
To delight in each number she pressed, instead of speed
Dialing on the mobile phone I wanted to be in her purse,

Or the possibility that she missed hearing the notes
Of the numbers, which perhaps to her were like a song
To hum in the shower, each tone a rung on a ladder

Of longing and sound, an overture to more promises.
But as I pulled into the Kwik Shop parking lot
It became clear that her tears were of a different kind.

She continued to cry *douze années, douze années,*
Douze années, repeating these twelve years far beyond
The poem I was pondering or the cigarettes I came to buy.

Twelve closed years that could only be placed
In a past spent pining after something that seemed
Certain. I found myself thinking strangely in twelve's:

Twice my married years; less than half my sudden age;
Disciples crucified upside down; double the hours a day
Requires in making up a life which, I read, we spend

50,000 hours dreaming away; and the number of months
That now fashion a year, thanks to certain Caesars. *Douze
Années*, she cried, so purely undone, and I simply watched

And listened, adjusting my rearview mirror to ensure that
What was behind me *was*, underwondering these twelve
Years in French I placed so tidily behind her; twelve

Years concluded with poignant precision at a Kwik Shop
Payphone. Years that, were there any tenderness left in a life
One can't call collect, could have added up differently.

Smoking Is Not an Activity

He is a banished man for a time
Because his wife hates cigarettes.

He tries to understand this as he sits
In the hallway's smoky exile feeling
Like Trotsky without an agenda.

And because "smoking is not an activity"
He makes it one, bringing books with him
To his Siberia of vapors. The neighbors

Can't understand it (nodding neighbors
Who dispense with adjectives), they briefcase
Past him, smile and speculate that his wife
Has allergies, or that there is a nightly
Misunderstanding that plants him

In the hallway smoking and reading,
His wife, perhaps, in the bath, surrounded
By scented candles. He thinks of when, long ago,
There were smoking rooms, and further back

In history no one read silently. You might have been
A heretic to do so, and what were you hiding anyway,
With only your eyes moving? It made people nervous
And poised to gather stones. And who knows?

In an undeciphered world perhaps you get what exile
You deserve. A hallway, a half-smoked cigarette,
A book by a dead man opened on your lap.

The Subtle Again

You expect something miraculous, something
Synesthetic to happen. But at first nothing happens.

Until you begin to notice your hands are empty,
The missing gesture of hand to mouth; you find

Only your wife has reason to touch your lips. You throw
Away your favorite ashtray (inexplicably washing it

Before putting it in the bin) and begin searching
For new ways to measure time; so many small moments

Suddenly need filling. Your wife sees in your decision
A moral victory, smells your hair at night for proof

Of your resolve and, in bed, articulates your burgeoning
Perfection: "You won't be a smoker anymore. Only

A man of will." You surmise you will begin to smell
The subtle again, and debate learning the names of flowers.

You wonder if, in a year's time, you'll become one of those
Characters in Victorian novels that always annoyed you.

The type of man that compliments and complements
The morning, drinks tea instead of coffee, and knows

The price of things. The sort of sad character that can look
At a flower, call it a rhododendron, and be perfectly correct.

The Golden Age of Good Times

"Can one point to a golden age of good times?"
—Stephen Dobyns

If we should all at once decide to try,
Like a group coup d'etat against states

Of sadness and regret, a revolution of gesture
Consisting of index fingers, human compass
Points trying for good and true norths,

How many of us could be found pointing
At one another, hoping to find so many
Welcome, reciprocal accusations?
(Knowing that this is how the world
Will end, not with bangs, whimpers,
Or any slouchings toward Bethlehem;
The world will end in hopeful indications.)

How many of the formerly, seemingly sad,
Confronted with such a charge, would be
Suddenly rendered happy, having only
To point the length of their front lawn?

And of the ones lucky enough to need
Only point to a photograph in a frame?
For the first time they would be envied
By all pointers except those too busy
Pointing at history or rebuttals
On page 9 of *The New York Times*.

And we'd reckon soon with those who,
Out of diffidence, persist in pointing
At their chins or their elbows, insisting,

Yes, this is the place, the very thing,
The good. Yes, here we come,

All of us, with our arms raised, our fingers
Extended, ultimately indicating everything;
We're strolling about our own Augustan
Romes, not surprised at all by how it was

So simply found amongst what were told,
But were never convinced, were ruins.

Business Lunch

I ask the table why,
In the 1940s, people
Looked at television,
Whereas today
People *watch*,
Realizing too late

That I've as much place
At this business lunch
As Wilde would
In an Alabama fraternity house.

And what with taxes due
And the price of copper down,
This is not the time to wonder
About how we fit our verbs;

Yet I can't help but notice
The participle *spending*
In the middle of the Lazy
Susan, hoping I choke
On something.

The God of Economic Utility
Passing me the salt.

Poet and Audience

I

THE ARGUMENT:
You Wondered Why You Weren't Published

It's because the postman has opened
All your submissions and kept them,
Tucked your words, as it were, under
His proverbial, federal wing.

And just so you know,
Your love poems *work*.
He reads them to his wife in bed
Before what has recently become
Most lyrical sex; he even adds

A few verbs here and there
For the sake of flow.

II

THE CONSOLATION

But you'll be pleased to know
He generally leaves your
Enjambment alone,
And understands well
The way irony goes;

A fulcrum for your failure
And his formally elegiac evenings,
Which he now has the diction
And courage to call *epiphanic*.

His only regret
Is that you ain't
More prolific.

We Read the Newspaper

For George W. Bush

It's true we envied of Jeff Chase
His Swiss Army knife
Full of gleaming diminutives:

Lilliputian saw and scissors;
Mysterious, sundry blades;
A plastic toothpick he actually used,
Removed and cool, as if waiting
To disdain through high noon.

And with the knife's miniature
Magnifying lens Jeff would harness
The sun, an anti-Prometheus for us
To wonder on as we huddled about him

Watching insects shrivel and smoke
Like things unbecoming. *The smoke
Looks like ribbons or souls,* he'd say.
The smoke that was their bodies.

The murdered that were never dissected.
That afternoon we watched him
Beat up Micah, threatening to cut him
Because his kind killed Christ.

Now, decades later, we read the newspaper;

And still we suffer nothing
In suffering all.

About the Type

This book was set in Perpetua, a type-face
Designed by the English artist Eric Gill,
And cut by the Monotype Corporation
Between 1928 and 1930. Perpetua is
A contemporary face of original design,
Without any historical antecedents.

The author of this collection of poems
Likewise has no historical antecedents,
But only because he's not well-read enough
To claim any. Having sampled Pound
In school, he's always trying to "make it new."
Who knew being ahistorical would pay off so well?

Mr. Gill, were he alive today, wouldn't have liked
What was done with his letters. Perpetua ruined
His marriage and later drove him to drink;
He'd have liked to think it had been worth it.

He'd hoped his letters would someday emboss
E.B. Browning or Elizabeth Bishop. He wanted
To help their words sit on the page like so
Many letter-pressed thrones. So please don't
Blame him for what he couldn't have known.

The readers who read *About the Type* would be
Wise to know that Eric Gill was not the type
Of man who wanted his font thrown about
Like confetti or favors; he labored for years
Over Perpetua (hence it's name) and he's not
To blame for the vertical clichés you're reading.

Were Mr. Gill to have his say, he'd ask that
The reader read these poems aloud and kindly
Leave him unnoticed; the reader should reckon
With the words, not his letters, which (it is written)
Are extremely elegant and form a most distinguished
Series of inscriptional letters—but not of words,
And certainly not of what words, in certain
Types of hands, have a habit of becoming.

Twelve Stanza Program

> "...man is the measure of all things..."
> —Protagorus

First, just under the title, I will place the correct
Quotation, book-ended with ellipsis, so my readers
Are certain I've read the Greeks before they begin

To watch me parade my first person as it conspicuously
Eats, takes walks, reads some haiku, contemplates
Bridges, has the occasional nightcap with Charles Mingus.

I will read the biography of a poet or a painter and later
Place Shelley in a discothèque, Vermeer watching
Reality Television, then sit back and watch the poems

Dance about the room, drunk on anachronism. I will
Gaze out any number of windows and chronicle
The movements of even those animals I don't see,

After which I'll peruse a book on orchids for hours
(Any ethos worth its salt is fluent in the language
Of flowers). A lost love will appear periodically

With a possibility in her proverbial pocket and a head
Full of obligatory hair that massages memory.
Even the moon isn't off limits to a first person like me.

I, for one, have seen it for the first time again and again
And, in order to round out this troublesome stanza,
I'll presume your passion for snow, the topography

Of clouds, rivulets, antique bridges, and field mice.
Mind, your knowledge of jazz must be as prodigious
As mine, and you must let me decide what it means

To quit smoking, to *truly* appreciate Pound, turn 50,
And above all you need to accept my mornings' lyrical
Minutiae, riddled with birdsong, coffee cups, and allusion.

You will slowly become convinced, when my artifice
Permits, that everything you've ever done, said, forgotten,
Or read had a poem in it you simply didn't notice. Your

Life, albeit full, has been too full of formless, almost
Moments that should have ended with action, with
Someone weeping or waving their way to becoming.

Your felt experience, like your participles, precariously
Dangling, perhaps preceded by the perfect adverb. *Listen.*
It's your lyrical, newly vertical life, passably singing.

III
Still Lives

Naming the Strange

> "...but here / within this thick black pelt,
> your strongest gaze / will be absorbed
> and utterly disappear."
> —Ranier Maria Rilke

Perhaps, in this perfunctory age, this is the closest
I will ever come to naming the strange. To run a bath,

Go downstairs for some coffee, come back, and find
My cat, King, in Bastet posture, sitting in the bathtub

Filling with warm water, indifferent that it is rising,
That she is sinking. And should I, at this late hour,

Wonder what it means to try and find suggestions
In such things? (Before long I'll start suspecting stop signs

Of subtext, duplicity of dial tones.) And regarding King,
I'm wondering if I still own the faith required to play

At Adam, give this strange similitude a name. Should I
Call my wife from the bedroom to also bear witness,

Or is this expectancy violation privately mine, a strictly
Local revelation? To give this scene some meat I'm afraid

I'm forced to fleece great minds again (in time everything
Is like something else, a variation on a viable theme;

This is the curse of a too good memory). My thoughts
Wander back to Rilke's Cat, and I decide that mine, too,

Has those silent, stoic, prehistoric eyes that can send us back.
It's time to admit that, to the cat, I am only another hairless ape:

A pair of wide eyes, a mouth agape at what I cannot name, create,
Or settle on without so many dead men's thoughts, murmuring.

Familiarity

"We experience things on a continuum, on a spectrum, that goes
from the most familiar to the most strange[...]. Familiarity is a scalar
phenomenon. Things are experienced by us as more or less familiar."
                                                    —John Searle

She woke up one morning confronting linearity.
By noon she was certain, with mid-twenties tenacity,
That the familiar was what made time slow. And now, newly
Thirty, and having read Kundera long ago, she is concerned

With lightness and weight, suspecting that even
The laws of gravity (things just seem *heavier*
Than they did at twenty-nine) have recognized her age.
She tells him over dinner that what we call "familiarity"

Is really a certain type of *slowness*, and that the symptoms
Are legion. "It's all in my mind," she said, "this malaise—
And in yours. Only now I have come to *doubt*." So
She's outlined a partial plan to combat the familiar.

The first step is that they occasionally give each other
New names, novel ways of reckoning with their domestic,
Pavlovian choreography. In order to be tourists of their own
Home most of the furniture will have to go, and to find

Their city buoyant and strange they will need to go to India
Soon. They will drink white wine instead of red, take baths
At night in lieu of morning showers, and revise their lives
Whenever repetition risks bordering on anything resembling

Belief, density, or languidness. The other night before bed
She called him "James" and asked about his day. He remembered
Her name for that week was "Lynn," said his day went so
Quickly, and got into his new side of the bed. "Good night,

James," she said. "Oh, I almost forgot. I want us to have a baby
Immediately and name it *Feather*—boy or girl. *Feather*, that is,
To begin with." He lay there and nodded at her feet, unfamiliarly
Touching the headboard; she sighed, turned her head and kissed

His ankle. The bedside clock that was no longer there
Would have read 5:30 P.M.; it was in the basement with
Their wedding photos, wine corks from memorable parties,
Formerly favorite novels, surrounded by other weighty relics.

Strongbox

You bought the box last week and now
We are filling it with the important things:
Car titles, birth certificates, letters
From the editor and every conceivable

Warranty. The man told you
It was indestructible, that should a fire
Break out of anywhere at any time
Our future would be fine. The box

Will seal itself at a certain temperature
And contain the truth that we were born,
Had insurance, a place to belong, and cars
In our names. All of this, he said, will survive

The flames. It's our time capsule, you said,
Our agreement with the inevitable, a warranty
Against time and what happens when
We move through it. And if it's true

That in this adult world every mistake
Is made by a professional, then we
Have a lunatic desire to turn up the heat
Just to *see*. We will, you tell me,

Have to make copies of the key, hide
One under the plant by the window,
Put the others on our key rings,
Sometime soon. Then, you assure me,

We can leave the house with the door open
Wide to the whole exploding world; we'll

Be busy mocking inferno and inevitability
With everything running. Feeling fireproof.

And for a time we'll confuse this with love.

Navigating the Dark

Papua, Indonesia

In this mining town in Papua the electricity
Has a habit of giving up at night, and this

Is a miracle of modern stasis, a secular Shabbat,
Reminding us of what is expendable, of how so few

Of us ever truly experience the dark. We are amazed,
My wife and I, with the heavy darkness

Of the no moon jungle, insect sounds lacerating
All illusions of silent places. "It's so absolute,"

My wife says, and I like to think she means
More than the darkness; the naked places

Of ourselves we dress in sunlight, lamps,
And recorded music like antithetical

Blanche DeBois's fearing a different sort
Of scrutiny. "We could pretend it's 1940,"

I say, "put a Jack Benny tape on the short wave
And drink coffee, light candles." She suggests

A walk outside instead, where there are dozens
Of others already out on paths bounded by jungle,

Stepping small and laughing loudly through various
Uncertainties; flashlights as eyes, ears like animals'.

Soon we are trying only to remember not to disappear
Altogether; everything is so absolutely, so darkly possible.

Arguments for Stillness

He knew that nouns made lonely in cities
Too full of verbs must *practice.*

So on nights it seemed that she didn't see him
He'd sit by the window and fancy himself

A sort of Hopper painting. It was the only way
He knew to make his loneliness less pitiable,

His solitude seem deliberate. Still, life alone framed
By the window felt too much like obviousness,

And he knew that in order to pull it off he needed
To be on the highest floor of a tall building

In a city that catered to anonymity, where he
Could look down at the people and the traffic,

High enough to know the inevitable symmetry
Of come and go. And somewhere outside the frame

He would conjure a watcher to watch him through
A metaphor shaped like a telescope, an artist

With the power to transcend the straightjackets
Of grammar, rendering him both subject and object:

The man in the window is the man in the window.
As far as arguments for stillness go, he'll do.

Ode

Five years of blood
Under the bridge and you
Respond via e-mail, the medium
I hate most, a reminder that the letter
Is dead. I read with my wife reading

Over my shoulder (this is how things
Happen now; the door's always open,
House lights on with the audience
Squinting), sitting on a hard chair reading

The screen. I mean to stop time someday,
Freeze us all mid-gesture and mood, give
Everyone a frame to frame themselves in.

Soon I'll begin to sift through my mythologies.
I'll rewind those parts where you appear,
Adjust the tracking so the image comes clear,
Sit down and write a letter of explanation

To you (still not *true*), but something
You can legend yourself through.

Lesson

He tells them of when, as a young man,
His now wife would write letters to him
From Sri Lanka on thin, blue airmail paper,

And how he would wait for them. Of her
Script pressed deep and hard on the page
(How he would hold her letters up

To the lamplight and watch her periods
Turn to stars), the stamps with pictures
Of otherworldly animals, princes,
And temples outside of time. How all
Available space was bedighted with words,
Jokes, and last minute musings wobbling up

The margins. How he would carry the letter
In his pocket until the next one arrived
As perspicacious proof that somewhere

He was pondered. How he would re-read them
When he was too happy for his own thoughts.
Of course the students don't know why

Their teacher is so emotional today, doubtless
Wondering if they should be taking notes (wanting
The half-life of this information, the estimated

Terminus of responsibility). The teacher
Tells them that if his thoughts are plagiaristic
He doesn't give a damn, and the reasons

Why McLuhan was *right*. The death
Of the letter is serious business; true sadness
Consists of those things you will never have

A chance to miss. Your life, he insists, will end
Up on your quiz; your life *is* the quiz. Please

Don't fuck this one up.

She Discovered the Dictionary

For Shari

She took the book to bed and read
(*Piezometry*) out loud, words
That I had heard before,
But now undressed, freed

From context and consequent sense.
Slicing through their roots, sliding
Down conjugations, she found

Herself laughing at the words
(*Piffle*), the ways her mouth moved
When uttering them, repeating

Them Stein-like (*pig*) until they
Were (*pig*) redeemable (*pig*)
Only through (*pig*) sound.

Words became qualified by new criteria:
Laughter, the spaces they left in the air,
Alliteration (*pig bed*), the assonance

Their neighbors made. She's taken
To fetching the book at parties, chancing
Muted faces (*pigboat*) and absurdity
For her (*pigeon*) words. And if the house

We're in doesn't have a dictionary
She uses my name instead, staring
At me, a glass of wine in her hand,

Repeating it *(Erik)* as the others watch on.
Soon he'll disappear! she says,
Watch and listen carefully. And I listen
To my staccato *(Erik)* christening, *(Erik)* sound,
Sans *(Erik)* fury, soon signifying *(Erik)* nothing.

Later, leaving the party, she tells me I'm lucky.
That although I've been *(Erik)* deconstructed,
My *(Erik)* phonemes, it seems, are endearing.

After Candlelight (12:30 A.M.)

After Billy Collins

It would have shocked Thoreau to see us earlier, candlelit,
Choosing to save the bottle of wine for a night somehow
More congruent than this. He'd have felt

Disconcerting waves of valuation, watching us go
Through our taxes by tapers at the kitchen table;
He could have guessed that, instead of making
Love, our modern sensibilities would find
Sense in taking this time to confront

Our inertia: the taxes, letters unwritten and unanswered,
The forgotten contents from the clutter drawer, all our
Mortal obligations exposed on the table, fanned
About us like magazines or the flickering
Semi-circle of a life under

Interrogation. It would have saddened him to see me forget
And keep trying the lights as I moved from room to room.
(My fingers, like so much of me now, an extension
Of choreographed expectation, resistant to
The slightest violation.) But by mid-

Night, the power still out, he might have been
Pleased to see me on the sofa reading by candlelight
A book written by a dead man who never knew electricity

But had his moments of lightning. I like
To think that Thoreau would have seen something
He recognized in my wife sleeping upstairs, her window
Open to cricket bows, or in my face when, at 12:15 A.M., I rose

As the radio resumed its song, mid-chorus,
And I squinted through this sudden world, small
With light, knocking over candles and wondering
Who needed this music; what fool left all of the lights on.

IV

East

Cambodia

I
To be an American is to learn

Geography by what you watch
CNN burn,

To later visit and take photos
Of all you didn't manage to destroy
Without thinking of Ozymandias.

To frame the photo of your wife
Posing behind a headless body
Made of sandstone. Her head

Where a smiling Buddha's
Used to be.

For posterity.

II
Driving a motorbike in Southeast Asia is Buddhism

There's an understanding of physics here
And the prevailing law
Is inertia:

If I am moving
And you are moving
We'd best let each other move.

The alternative is traffic lights, more
Unnatural laws to master.

III
What the novice monk said in answer to the question:
"Have you found yourself?"

Yes,
I'm right here.

For now.

IV
Ankor Thom

This is the place where language fails,
And with no articulation left, you can

Only laugh small laughs, politely
Covering your mouth,
Hilariously incapable of the ancient.

V
Last thoughts on war, Cambodia 2003

There are some sins
So egregious
That they can create
A god,

He said, looking
At a pile of skulls.

Nobody heard him. No
Body prayed.

VI
Road sign in Phnom Penh that may very well explain everything

SLOWLY MAN IS WORKING

Nick Asks *Do You Meditate*, Leaving the Question Mark Off

This is not the sort of filtered factuality
My former student, Nick, needs:
My first Buddhist monk chatting on
A laptop in the Colombo airport,

Or the quiet confessions that accompany
Bad backs and tinnitus (it can take years
To become your own worst anachronism).
And my back is reminding me that Nick

Is still young enough not to have his Kyoto
Assaulted by cameraed tourists and smoking
Roshis; he's still reading Kerouac,
On the precipice of Hesse and more

Conspicuous austerities. How to answer him
Now suspecting that, despite years in Thailand
And meeting Ginsberg twice, we are not
All beautiful in song? And if I saw the Buddha

On the side of the road I still wouldn't kill
Him, but I wouldn't give him a lift either,
Too worried that the abstraction riding
Shotgun had more than a koan or a flower

Sermon hidden in the folds of his robes—
A pistol, a tax return, perhaps a worn copy
Of *The Portable Nietzsche* that, when opened,
Makes him a grow a moustache before

Disappearing. Or better still, a small bell
Without a clapper that he shakes serenely,
Seeing as silence can mean anything
In the right man's hands. My reply,

Nick, is this (all metaphors exposed, things
Almost what they are): one hand shaking
A small bell, not clapping.

Object Lesson

For my students

Had I a little better Buddha in me I'd not have been
So silly with questions of Hamlet's madness,

Or with defending Hemingway's characters, which,
I'd finally be fit to admit, always sound like Hemingway.

I'd have been more self-evident, certainly, had I
Not been so silly with answers, or too busy

Citing history, fearing words needed thrones,
Pyramids or Corinthian columns to buttress them

Against those young hands, a field of silent fingers
Raised which, it seemed to me then, were poised only

To challenge ideas down. I shouldn't have answered
So hastily those students who needed better questions,

Those few who, heavy with hope, wondered what
Is beauty, knew their Huxley, and earnestly asked:

What if this world is *another planet's Hell?* Had I then
A better Buddha in me I could have come to class

Prepared with lotus flowers in my briefcase in lieu
Of more words neatly arranged like insight. I'd have

Placed one flower on each student's desk and waited;
I would have asked them one by one if the flower

On their desk filled them with fury. After this I'd have
Been able to end my lessons with just enough objective

Reality; free enough to have had them hand in their blank,
No word essays. Not stapled, but folded neatly. Like origami.

The Magic Mountain

"Seven years Hans Castorp remained
amongst those up there."
—Thomas Mann

I finished it in Chiang Mai, Thailand,
After eleven months of chilies, rice, and rain,

Thinking Mann knew me, like Salinger did
At age fifteen, all the anger, so much *try*
In the right places.

For me it was university Mann conjured,
Marcos, my Settembrini, strangely tubercular,
Pontificating sadly toward glory.

Sean had to be my Naptha telling me about grace,
It's in His face, he'd say, and I'd light another
Cigarette as identically sad as Hans Castorp
Wasn't and should have been. And later

When the winter came to the West
I knew that the snow was a metaphor,
Something to get lost in, something easy

To underwonder (there was no blanket warmth
In Thailand and I'd ponder this on the streets
Of Chiang Mai, a tuk-tuk choking by reminding

Me of movement, of heat) thinking of us then,
A dirty apartment full of deconstructions,
All the windows festooned with Aeolian harps.

Who will stop by and what should we drink,
And think of all the books that need reading.
The need to not leave, to make every verb a noun,

To sit perfectly still and watch the snow fall.
The smallest movement could startle us all
Into moving.

At 6:15 P.M. in Chiang Mai, Thailand

The mayflies hatch and rise
Like bubbles blown beneath
My balcony, and because life
Is monstrous the birds become

Monsters. Hundreds of them
Waiting in the palms,
Then swooping and gulping
While I am trying

To write a poem about love
But can't for the chirping
And the sound of snapping beaks.

I try to follow a mayfly with my eye,
Betting on its probability, making it
Into all of man's choices and chances.

But my fly is no trooper and never makes it
Far up or away, and I'd like this to mean
That there may be more to this scene,
A method in the monstrous.

The next day I hear a Thai man say:
Mayfly mean rain comes soon.
I love sweeping those little wings.

But it is sad, too.

Mysterious Farang*

Because she worries
About his motivations and why,

At night, he habitually drops
His keys in the hall, my wife

Is investigating our neighbor,
The Mysterious Farang. She plans

To collect the *Bangkok Posts* that he
Leaves like bled corpses outside his door

(We decided to read them one night,
Pinch them since we were poor,
And found holes in the paper, squares
Of anti-news there); she suggests

We budget, skip the afternoon's rice,
Buy the paper each night and match

The holes in his with the wholeness
Of ours in order to discover his penchants,

Where his mind meets his scissors,
What he pauses for.

Before long, she tells me,
I'll be holding his keys!

Then we'll be free
To move on to larger mysteries.

* *Farang* – "Foreigner of European descent" in phonetic Thai.

Dead Man's Wallet

When waiting for anything or to fill in
The silent spaces standing in any kind of line,
I'll open my wallet and pretend it's a dead man's
Because I'm always trying to make the familiar

Strange. I stumbled across him reeking in the jungle
This morning; I hid the body safely, buried beneath the palms.
This time I didn't mind the money I suspected wasn't there,
Satisfied enough with knowing this man's name and what photos

He carried (all easily explained), and I already surrounded
His ticket stub from 1994 with a story about love ending
Sadly. The picture of Bela Lugosi, I'll admit, still troubles me
With possibility, but I think it connotes a man of complexity,

An artist type, a detective of himself who was, at one point,
Upset that *The Paris Review* never responded, that no one
Ever photographed him in black and white while he was brooding
Or writing in his study with smoke (there simply *must* be smoke)

Curling about his head like so many un-tethered, ghostly
Thoughts. Such a photo, surely, would have been in his wallet
Had it existed. It has been four or five hours since I buried the body,
And I don't feel suspicious or in any way wrong, but happy

In knowing that I would certainly be more missed than this man
Had I disappeared in the jungle. The man holding *my* wallet
Would hear sirens; have to face my face on posters and television.
Soon enough, I'd like to think, he'd have to answer tough questions.

Cat, Man, God

"Our cats like god have never spoken
a word that wasn't ours."
                    —Stephen Dunn

My brother phones from Nebraska for the first time
In six months, undone that his cat is dead. He says
It's different from when his wife left. The cat

Wasn't addicted to OxyContin and never sold the sofa
While he was at work. It only wanted warmth
And soft places; it slept with him for seven years.

Assholes hate cats, he maintains, because they're afraid
Of silent, warm spaces. They're terrified

Of what they would and what they wouldn't
Find if they stared out the window for hours.

Every cat is a sphinx, he says,
Devouring time.

                    *

In ancient Egypt, of course, the cat was sacred.

But in the Cairo Museum there are cats
Wrapped behind glass, bred, I read,
Solely for mummification. Still,
Born to be immortal.

*

A photograph my friend took at the Coliseum
In Rome: a white tomcat in the foreground, backlit
And regal; the Coliseum in the background, blurred.

On the back of the photo is written:
Render unto Caesar what is Caesar's?
The *cats* rule the ruins of Rome.
There is a lesson here somewhere.

*

And tonight, my cat, King, born in the jungles
Of Papua and fond of water, had a baby gecko
Cornered by the bathroom scale.

The gecko had defensively dropped its tail,
Which persisted to writhe just north
Of its head like something forgotten,
Like rootless punctuation
For an idea that came
Too suddenly or too late.

And it took a strange strength
To see this for what it was
Without wishing.

The cat's paw on the gecko's fetus-like,
White belly. The cat's eyes wide
And deliberate (admit it) being
Precisely what she was.

The Pharaoh Speaks

"Very big. Very old."
—A tour guide describing the pyramids of Giza

Call them slaves or selfless subjects
Building for faith or fiat. I don't give
A mummified shit for semantics

Or motivations so long as they are
Stacking stone. I alone am
The unmovable object, the infinite

North, halving horizons.
It's not death, but the wonderers
I'm preparing for. Time abhors

Man's buildings of wood, its paper
Plans, and every humble man's
Orisons. History's finishing jest

Is this: she always forgives
Man's extravagances; she celebrates
The shameless in song. Time

Is *long*. Your smooth economies
Will go unnoticed. In time
Everything still standing is forgiven.

Epilogue:

Considering Something Aristotle Said

Papua, Indonesia

Moments ago I was, perhaps, feeling
Too insouciant, like I belonged
Among the privileged few

Who have too much time to sit
On a balcony overlooking
A jungle full of trees
That they can't name,
And so can truly see.

It was soon after this that I became lazy

With my thoughts and began proving
What we truly are: walking habits
In creature form, our daily designs
Fitting so faithfully we forget
To pause at mirrors and make
Comparisons.

For a moment I understood the nameless

Argonauts whose only glory was to row,
Who never minded coming home
Again and again after each re-telling

With arms fleeceless and empty
Because that's how Apollonius of Rhoades
Rendered them: mute rowers, ill equipped
To argue with mythology, accustomed
To their lives' unheralded, lateral moves.

Lazily I put down my book wondering if I knew

How to make the Sheppard's Pie I promised
My wife for dinner; I reached for my lighter
And, with the flame an inch from my nose,
Realized I hadn't a cigarette in my mouth,
And I remembered that this is because

Of another Greek I read, something
Aristotle said concerning character

Being a question of cumulative habit.
And if this is so, I supposed, touching,
Like Thomas, the tip of my nose,

There must be scores of us sad characters out there.

Enough of us to play the most predictable game
Of checkers ever played, certainly enough of us
To compose a small army of redundant souls
Only capable of seizing castles that anticipate
Their falls. And instead of flexing my most

Purposeful pose or quitting something
I'm ashamed I enjoy or walking straight
Into the jungle, barefoot, to test its legends
Or finally moving my desk to the sunlit side
Of my study, I went inside to find my Marlboros
And smoked two in a row, using, because of Aristotle,

My left hand instead of my right. My left
Hand, I reckoned, would never see it coming;
It would think something strangely new, something

Out of character was happening. My fingers
Twitchy, ready to welcome this minute mutiny.

Born in Omaha, Nebraska in 1972, Erik Campbell lives in Papua, Indonesia, where, for the last four years, he hasn't worked very hard as a technical writer for an American mining company. His poems and essays have appeared in *The Iowa Review*, *Tin House*, *The Virginia Quarterly Review*, *The Massachusetts Review*, *Gulf Coast*, *Rattle*, and other journals. He has never won a literary award, but he does have a snappy collection of antique typewriters and comic books, both of which are currently languishing in his in-laws basement in Elwood, Nebraska. He hopes to retrieve them someday.